Frilled Lizard or Frilled Neck Lizard

Pet Lizards

Facts on Frilled Lizard, Frilled Dragon, purchasing, caring, diet, feeding, habitat, breeding.
A Completer Owner's Guide, in color.

By Les O. Tekcard

Disclaimer

Although the author and publisher have made every effort to ensure that the information in this book was correct at press time, the author and publisher do not assume and hereby disclaim any liability to any party for any loss, injury, damage or disruption caused by errors or omissions, whether such errors or omissions result from negligence, accident, non-functional websites, or any other cause. Any advice or strategy contained herein may not be suitable for every individual.

ISBN : 978-0-9923922-8-4

Printed by Lightning Source, Victoria

Foreword

(Please note that you will see many variations of the common names of this lizard used in the text. Frill Necked, Frilled Neck, and Frill Neck among other variations are all used and are all considered to be correct, as are Frill Dragon and Frilled Dragon among others.)

Dinosaurs fascinate us, perhaps stirring some primordial memory in our brains from the days when these behemoths dominated the planet and men cowered in their shadows.

Whether it's on the screen in films like *Jurassic Park*, or on the living room rug in a riot of children's plastic toys, it's hard for any of us to resist the pull of these now extinct giants.

Reports of living dinosaurs always generate interest and speculation. Is there a beast in Scotland's Loch Ness that has survived for thousands of years? Could others like him (or her) live in the deepest ocean or hidden in a remote jungle?

While cryptozoologists run around looking for proof that such mythic creatures dwell hidden among us today, there is a species of lizard indigenous to Australia quietly existing as a veritable latter-day dinosaur – the Frill Neck Lizard.

Some adults of this species reach a length of 3 feet (0.9 m), and are arguably both bizarre and impressive. They have the ability to open a cape-like flap of skin that normally hangs around their shoulders into a full, pleated ruff or frill that fans out around their heads.

At the same time, they open their mouths to reveal a vivid yellow coloration, while letting out a convincing and chilling hiss as part of their elaborate threat display.

Since these lizards are also capable of standing on their hind legs and running upright, they can be downright terrifying to encounter, even though they are docile, and quite receptive to handling when socialized from an early age.

I will never forget the awe in one little boy's voice when he saw his first Frill Neck Lizard, "Is it a dragon?" he asked in a whisper. "Can you make it breathe fire?"

While you won't see smoke coming from a Frilled Neck Lizard's nostrils, or flames shooting from its mouth, you can understand how a child would look at this strange animal and imagine it to be a storybook creature come to life or a dinosaur reincarnated.

Frill Necked Lizards are not, however, children's pets. They are highly specialized reptile companions with specific needs in terms of diet and habitat. Although carnivorous in the wild, they will thrive on insects in captivity if given a varied diet and supplied with vitamin and calcium supplementation.

Only experienced reptile enthusiasts should keep this species and then only if they can supply adequate room for the animals to be housed safely. Frill Neck Lizards are arboreal. They live in trees in the wild, and they do require vertical spaces to be both healthy and happy. You might be able to keep a young Frill Neck in a standard aquarium, but the arrangement won't last for long.

For these reasons, a Frilled Neck Lizard should never be an impulse purchase, no matter how fascinated you are with their unusual looks and interesting, curious personalities.

Never opt for one of these creatures as a pet until you have taken the time to learn the correct facts about Frilled Lizards in order to make a truly informed decision about how one will fit into your life and that of your family.

Presumably, that is why you have purchased and are reading this book. Hopefully, by the end of the text, you will have a solid understanding of the husbandry needs of this species, and a good sense of your own ability to care for a Frilled Neck Lizard.

If you have any doubts, don't make the purchase! Remember that a living creature will be dependent on the choices and decision you make. Always proceed with care and real concern for the animal itself when you choose a pet of any kind.

The first responsibility perspective animal parents have is to make a wise decision, even if that decision is, "No, I can't keep this animal appropriately at this time."

If, however, you finish this book and do move forward in your plan to keep a Frill Neck Lizard, I can promise you that you will be sharing your life with a fascinating, once-in-a-lifetime kind of pet.

NOTE: Please do not think that a Frilled Neck Lizard is a pet that can be kept in a small aquarium for life. While this kind of limited housing may be fine for a hatchling, or even a juvenile, it won't work for a full-grown adult.

In fact, many health complications can develop from keeping a Frill Necked Lizard in a space that is not large enough for its needs. For these reasons, we are not talking about a type of pet that will work well for apartment dwellers.

Acknowledgments

I would like to extend my sincerest thanks to my friends and family who supported me throughout this journey. I'd like to thank my wife especially for her patience with me throughout my research and writing – thank you, mySweetheart!!

Table of Contents

Table of Contents

Table of Contents

Table of Contents

Chapter 1 – Introducing the Frilled Lizard

Frilled Lizards are known by several different names including Frill Neck Lizard, Frilled Dragon and even King Lizard. These lizards are native to Australia and southern New Guinea where they can be found lounging in trees in their natural habitat.

All you have to do is look at Frilled Neck Lizard pictures like the one above to see why these creatures are so highly recognizable. They were featured on the Australian 2-cent coin for many years and are commonly depicted in cartoons. In recent years, they have also become popular as a household pet.

The Frilled Lizard is a very interesting species and it can be quite a joy to keep as a pet. Like all pets, however, there are a number of responsibilities that come with owning one of these lizards.

In order to keep your lizard happy and healthy you will need to provide it with a proper enclosure, a healthy diet and routine healthcare.

In this book you will find all the information you need to care for your Frilled Lizard as well as answers to some of the most commonly asked questions new lizard owners have. With this book in hand, you will become an expert in practically no time!

Before you go out and purchase a Frilled Lizard as a pet, you need to learn a thing or two about them. This involves more than the basic care instructions.

You should have an overall understanding of how these lizards exist in their native environment so you can create the ideal captive habitat for them at home.

They are much more active than you may think, and they need as much vertical as horizontal space

In this chapter you will learn the basics about Frilled Lizards as a species including where they come from, what they look like and their history as pets.

1.) What Are Frilled Lizards?

The Frilled Lizard (*Chlamydosaurus kingii*) belongs to the family *Agamidae*. This family contains more than 300 species of lizards, many commonly called dragons or dragon lizards.

Some of the other well-known species found in this family include the bearded dragon and *Uromastyx* species. Though bearded dragons are more commonly seen in the pet trade, the Frilled Lizard has gained more popularity as a companion species in recent years.

Frilled Lizards are reptiles known for their prehistoric appearance. They are native to northern Australia and southern New Guinea, and easily identified by the large frill around their necks.

The frill typically stays folded against the neck, but can be extended as a warning to predators or to rival males. These lizards tend to inhabit warm climates, living primarily in trees.

As you can imagine, the name Frilled Lizard comes from the distinctive neck, but you will see the same creatures referred to as frill neck lizard, frilled dragon and King's lizard.

The Frilled Lizard has played a role in popular culture in a variety of ways. Most significantly, it appeared on the Australian 2-cent coin until 1991 and was the mascot for the 2000 Paralympic Games.

Frilled Lizards have also been featured in film and television in titles like *The Rescuers Down Under* (Disney) and *Totally Wild*.

After the film *Jurassic Park* was made in 1993, frilled lizards became even more popular due to their resemblance to the prehistoric dinosaur the dilophosaur, which is featured prominently in a scene in the movie.

The dilophosaur also had a frilled neck, and a group of them are responsible for killing the computer programmer, Dennis Nedry, who was making money smuggling embryos off the island.

Frilled Lizards are a much smaller and considerably less dangerous version of the dilophosaur, which lived 193 million years ago and was 23 feet / 7 meters long and weighed in at 1,100 to 2,220 lbs. / 500 to 1000 kg!

They also do NOT spit nasty venom when they're angry, which is a definite plus in a pet!

2.) Facts About Frilled Lizards

Still, the Frilled Lizard is a fairly large species, growing up to 3 feet (0.9 m) in length. The ruff of skin (or frill) that sits around the neck hangs over the back like a cape.

When extended, however, it can reach up to 12 inches (30 cm) across and is used for communication or as a means of scaring off predators. In many cases, the lizard opens its frill when it is startled.

At the same time, the creature will also open its mouth in a menacing fashion and let out a very scary and menacing hissing sound.

Frilled lizards are typically gray or brown in coloring in order to remain camouflaged in the trees where they live. The inside of the frill is colored, however, as is the inside of the mouth.

These areas will be yellow or pink to add to the visual effect of the lizard's threat display. The frill itself opens in a pleated fashion, which gives the lizard the appearance of a much greater physical size.

One of the most interesting facts about this species is that it is capable of bipedal locomotion – standing and running on two legs. The sight of a Frill Neck Lizard running upright on two legs without question ads to the bizarre appearance of these already unique creatures, and is completely unforgettable!

Bipedalism is seen in other kinds of lizards as well, but the Frill Necks are unique. Other lizards can only run upright at high rates of speed, but the Frill Neck can maintain the posture at a variety of speeds because he can pull his body farther back while upright.

This superior ability to achieve and maintain balance is actually one of the Frilled Neck Lizard adaptations directly related to the frill itself. As the frill became larger over successive generations, the lizards' necks also became longer, which shifted their center of gravity backward over the hips. This shift allowed them to learn how to stand upright and once having done so, to vary the angle so they can walk upright at varying rates of speed.

Frilled "dragons" as they are sometimes called spend about 90% of their time in the wild hanging on to tree trunks 6.56 – 9.84 feet (2-3 meters) off the ground. They stay in this position to watch their territory for something to catch and eat.

When the lizard sees a likely meal, he jumps down and runs over to snatch up the item, then returns to his spot in the tree. Some naturalists have argued that this behavior means the Frill Necked Lizard isn't truly arboreal, but just using a tree as a roost while actually hunting on the ground.

That seems like splitting hairs, since these creatures prefer to be near trees, and crave the same kind of vertical space when kept in captivity. In the wild, however, individual lizards won't stay in one tree for more than a day at a time, probably because they want to stay one step ahead of their prey.

If the Frilled Neck were to stay in one spot all the time, the animal they eat would start to avoid that location pretty quickly!

Wild Frilled Lizards are carnivorous, eating a combination of insects, spiders and other small lizards. In captivity, however, they are largely insectivorous, feeding on a diet of insects supplemented with the occasional pinkie mouse.

Because these lizards are ectothermic, they rely on the temperature of their environment to regulate the temperature of their bodies.

They can be docile pets if they are handled routinely from an early age, and they are appealing as companions due to their long lifespan, which can be as much as 20 years.

3.) Summary of Facts

- **Scientific Classification**: *Chlamydosaurus kingii*
- **Other Names**: frill neck lizard, frilled dragon, King's lizard
- **Native Environment**: northern Australia and southern New Guinea
- **Natural Habitat**: humid climates, forests and savannahs
- **Size**: grows up to 3 feet (0.9 m) in length
- **Temperament**: can be tamed with frequent handling from a young age
- **Lifespan**: about 20 years
- **Other Pets**: should not be kept with other lizards
- **Diet:** primarily insectivorous in captivity

- **Reproduction**: breed during the spring after 2-month period of brumation, the reptilian equivalent of mammalian hibernation
- **Average Clutch Size**: 6 to 8, can be up to 11 eggs

4.) History of Frilled Lizards as Pets

Prior to the 1960s, little information about the Frilled Lizard was available. This creature was rare outside of its native habitat and it was even rarer to successfully breed one in captivity.

Today, however, these lizards are becoming increasingly common as pets and they are captive bred in large numbers. Not only are they popular, but populations in their native habitats continues to remain stable ensuring their survival as a species.

5.) Types of Frilled Lizards

Though there is only one species of Frilled Lizard, there are two different varieties – the Australian Frilled Lizard and the New Guinea Frilled Lizard.

In Australia, Frilled Lizards are most common in the Northern territory. In New Guinea, Frilled Lizards are farmed in the western half of the island which belongs to Indonesia.

Australia does not allow for exportation of the Frilled Lizard, so all specimens available in the United States are captive-bred. New Guinea Frilled Lizards, however, are likely hatched in their native land and imported into the U.S.

There is no official color or pattern for the Frilled Lizard, though certain colorations are more common depending on the region from which the lizard comes.

In Queensland, for example, Frilled Lizards commonly exhibit yellow-patterned skin with black and white markings. In the Northern Territory, the skin may be closer to orange in color with red, black and white markings.

The coloration may also vary according to the climate in which the lizards live. Specimens living in damper regions have darker colors to serve as effective camouflage in the trees native to the area.

Some of the predators that threaten Frill Necked Lizards in the wild include larger lizards, owls, eagles, snakes, quolls, and dingoes.

In order to provide your Frilled Lizard with the ideal habitat in captivity, you need to know where it comes from. Captive-bred specimens are more adaptable to a variety of living conditions, while wild-caught specimens are likely to be pickier about their habitat.

Just be sure to do your research before you buy a lizard so you know what to provide in the way of appropriate habitat and husbandry considerations.

Chapter 2 – What to Know Before Your Buy

Now that you know the basics about the Frilled Lizard as a species, you can begin to think more about owning one as a pet. Don't be too eager, however, because there is still more to think about.

Do you need a license to keep a Frilled Lizard in your area? How many should you buy? And what are the pros and cons of Frilled Lizards as pets? You will learn the answers to these questions and more in this chapter.

1.) Do You Need a License?

When it comes to keeping exotic animals as pets, you always need to be careful about licensing requirements.

Certain species are protected by law and are illegal to keep, regardless of permits.

Before you go and buy a Frilled Lizard you need to make sure that it is legal to do so in your area. You also need to determine whether or not a permit is required.

a.) Licensing in the U.S.

In the United States there are two legislative acts you have to worry about when it comes to licensing reptiles – the United States Endangered Species Act (ESA) and the Convention on International Trade in Endangered Species of Wild Fauna and Flora (CITES).

These acts regulate the importation of live animals as well as animal products and are designed to protect endangered and threatened species from exploitation. Luckily, the Frilled Lizard is considered neither endangered nor threatened so it is not affected by these pieces of legislation.

In regard to state regulations, permits are generally only required for keeping endangered or threatened species as well as native species of reptile.

For example, in Ohio you are only allowed to keep a total of four individuals from certain lists of wild-caught native species. The Frilled Lizard is not native to the United States and, therefore, its keeping is loosely regulated. To be sure you do not require a permit to keep a Frilled Lizard in your area, contact your state's game department.

As a word of advice, the more information you can supply to the authorities about the lizard you plan to keep, its diet, and behavior, the more likely you will be to avoid legal complications.

With exotic animals, it often falls to the prospective owner to educate the correct offices about the animal's safety since in all likelihood, they will have no direct experience with the species in question.

b.) Licensing in the United Kingdom

In the United Kingdom, the major piece of legislation you have to worry about is the Animal Welfare Act. This legislation was passed in 2006, placing a duty of care on pet owners to ensure the responsible keeping of animals.

The law requires that pet owners provide a suitable environment and diet for their animals as well as making provisions for the creature to be able to exhibit normal behavior and to live free of pain and suffering.

Though the Animal Welfare Act regulates the care of pets in the UK, it does not require the licensing of reptiles like the Frilled Lizard. In fact, there are no licensing requirements in the UK for reptiles or amphibians unless they are endangered or dangerous.

To make sure you do not need a license in your particular area, contact your local council. Again, be prepared with all the facts about your lizard so you can accurately answer any questions that are raised.

c.) Licensing in Australia

Because Frilled Lizards are native to Australia, licensing requirements may differ from other nations. It is illegal to take Frilled Lizards from the wild, but they can be kept as pets with the proper permit in all the states except Tasmania and Western Australia. To inquire about permits in your area, contact the Office of Environment and Heritage.

Keep in mind that, in Australia, Frilled Lizards require a Class 2 license for species that are considered rare, dangerous or difficult to keep. These licenses are only available for individuals 18 years or older who have at least 2 years of experience caring for Class 1 reptiles. Class 1 reptiles include the eastern water dragon, eastern bearded dragon, eastern snake-necked turtle, common bluetongue lizard, children's python and the carpet python.

2.) How Many Should You Buy?

The number of Frilled Lizards you buy depends on how much space you can provide for them. These lizards require at least 4' x 3' x 6' (1.2 x 0.9 x 1.82 meters) of space because they are very active and can grow up to 3 feet in length (0.91 m).

If space is not an issue, you can house two or more Frilled Lizards in the same cage as long as they are not both male. Males are bound to fight, though two females or a single male and single female can live together peacefully.

3.) Can Frilled Lizards Be Kept with Other Pets?

Frilled Lizards are a very active species and can be somewhat tempestuous at times. This being the case, they need plenty of space to themselves and they generally do not do well with other species.

Inexperienced owners sometimes make the mistake of thinking that Frilled Lizards can be housed with bearded dragons due to their similar native environment and heat requirements.

This is not recommended, however. You should also keep in mind that Frilled Lizards may eat smaller lizards so it is best to house them only with others of their own kind.

4.) Ease and Cost of Care

Though they were once considered quite rare, Frilled Lizards are now fairly popular as pets. Along with their popularity comes a wealth of information regarding their care and keeping. Thanks to all of this information, it is generally not difficult to keep a Frilled Lizard as a pet.

You do, however, need to make sure to provide for your pet's basic needs including a suitable Frilled Necked Lizard habitat, a healthy diet and access to proper care. As long as you provide these basics, you should have little trouble with your Frilled Lizards.

Part of being a pet owner involves assuming the financial responsibility of caring for your animals. Frilled Lizards require a fairly large enclosure, a diet of many different insects, and routine veterinary care.

All of these factors and more contribute to the total cost of keeping a Frilled Lizard as a pet.

In this section you will learn about the initial costs of buying and preparing to bring a Frilled Lizard into your life, as well as the monthly costs to keep one properly.

Understanding these costs before you bring your lizard home will help you to be more prepared for the needs of these unique creatures.

5.) Initial Costs

The initials costs for keeping a Frilled Lizard as a pet include both the acquisition of the animal itself, and the design and decoration of its habitat, which is typically a glass aquarium.

a.) Purchase Price

The purchase price of your Frilled Lizard will vary depending where you get it. Generally, however, the cost for a hatchling ranges between $100 and $150 (£65 to £97.50.)

b.) Enclosure

Again, the cost of your Frilled Lizard's enclosure will depend where you get it. You may be able to find a 30-gallon tank for about $100 (£65), but it is often difficult to get one with the correct dimensions without paying for a custom-built unit.

Many Frilled Lizard owners choose to purchase or build a custom enclosure to ensure that they are meeting their pet's needs. The cost for a custom enclosure can range from $200 and $1000 (£130 to £650) depending on size and materials.

The Internet is a treasure trove of information on designing custom pet enclosures. I recommend that you use your favorite search engine and look for "custom reptile tank" or "custom reptile enclosure."

Go to the "images" option for the search, and you will be able to browse pictures of these one-of-a-kind habitats. If you are a "do it yourself" type or know someone who is, you may be able to shave hundreds of dollars off the cost of an enclosure.

What is most important, however, is providing your lizards with an environment they will love and in which they will thrive.

c.) Tank Decorations

In order to make your Frilled Lizard comfortable in his new home you will need to decorate the space with a number of wooden structures and branches. The cost for these items is not terribly significant, generally around $50 (£32.50).

Again, the Internet can give new lizard owners a wealth of ideas about making their pet's habitat as natural as possible.

d.) Heating and Lighting

Two of the most important elements in your Frilled Lizard's tank are the heating and lighting. These elements will affect your lizard's health and wellbeing so you do not want to skimp on these items.

Be sure to purchase a proper UVB light that is designed for use with reptiles as this will help your pet to produce and synthesize the correct levels of Vitamin D3. A 12-hour cycle of light and dark is recommended, so a lamp with a timer attachment can be very useful.

Lizards enjoy one area of the cage that is specifically set aside for basking. This spot will be hotter than other parts of the habitat and should reach at least 95 and 102°F (35 to 39°C).

Other areas of the habitat should be kept at around 75 to 80°F (23 to 26°C) during the day and should not be allowed to drop lower than 72-75 F / 22.2-25.5 C at night, which is why an under-the-tank heater is also a necessity. The relative humidity in the tank should be kept at 55-65%.

The easiest way to monitor internal conditions in your lizard's habitat is to buy a thermometer / hygrometer combination at a cost of about $5-$10 / £3-£6 for an analog unit. I personally prefer a digital model like Fluker's Digital Display Thermo-Hygrometer for $20 / £12.

The Fluker device is easy to read and has the advantage of showing both Celsius and Fahrenheit temperature numbers.

Because the box is small and compact, it also won't detract from the appearance of the habitat. Your lizards won't care what it looks like, but you probably will!

The cost of lamps and heaters varies widely as there are so many sizes and levels of quality for this kind of equipment. In general, you should be able to find what you need at an expense of $100 to $300 (£65 to £195).

e.) Other Equipment

Some of the other items you will need to purchase initially include food and water bowls, a water bottle to mist the enclosure, and substrate to line the bottom of the tank.

The cost for these items should average under $50 (£32.50.)

f.) Summary of Initial Costs

Cost Type	One Lizard	Two Lizards
Purchase Price	$100 to $150 (£65 to £97.50)	$200 to $300 (£130 to £195)
Enclosure	$100 to $1000 (£65 to £650)	$100 to $1000 (£65 to £650)
Tank Decorations	$50 (£32.50)	$50 (£32.50)
Heating and Lighting	$100 to $300 (£65 to £195)	$100 to $300 (£65 to £195)
Other Equipment	$50 (£32.50)	$50 (£32.50)
Total:	$400 to $1550 (£260 to £1008)	$500 to $1700 (£325 to £1105)

6.) Monthly Costs

In addition to the initial costs of purchasing and preparing for your Frilled Lizard to become a member of your household, you also need to consider the costs of your pet's monthly upkeep.

Some of the ongoing costs to be considered are the expenses associated with food, supplements, substrate, veterinary care, and repairs or replacements for the cage and cage decorations.

Below you will find an explanation of the expenses for each of these items as well as a table detailing the total monthly cost for these aspects of your lizard's care.

a.) Food (Insects)

The price for feeder insects depends what type you buy and where you buy them. In the pet store, you are likely to pay higher prices than you would ordering in bulk online.

For example, a pet store might charge $20 (£13) for 200 crickets while an online supplier would sell as many as 1000 for the same price.

Because Frilled Lizards subsist almost entirely on insects you should be prepared to purchase a large quantity of several different varieties. For reference sake, budget about $30 to $50 (£19.50 to £32.50) per month for food.

b.) Supplements

In addition to feeder insects, you will also need to keep a regular supply of multi-vitamin powder and calcium supplements.

You will need to dispense these supplements once or twice a week, usually by dusting the feeder insects with a powdered preparation.

One bottle of supplement will last several weeks so you shouldn't need to spend more than $15-$20 (£9.75 / £12) per month.

c.) Substrate

The cost of substrate will vary depending what type you use and how often you clean out your Frilled Lizard's cage. The major concern is that you not use anything that your pet will eat that will cause it to develop an impaction in the digestive tract.

Good substrate options include potting soil, which is very economical, selling for approximately $10 /£7 per cubic foot / .028 cubic meters. (Make sure the soil is fertilizer and pesticide free.)

Coconut fiber can also be used, and works well since it doesn't tend to develop mold growth. Twenty-four quarts / 22.7 liters of coconut fiber can be purchsed for $17-$20 / £10.25-£13.

Bricks of substrate by Bed-A-Beast have proven to be popular, as has play sand. Some enthusiasts prefer to line their lizard's habitat with non-adhesive shelf liner, reptile carpet, or layers of either paper towels or newspaper. (There is no need to be concerned about the ink as most papers now use soya based ink products.)

You can even opt for Cyprus mulch, readily available at big box gardening and home repair stores for as little as $3.80 / £2.25 per 2 cubic feet / 0.56 cubic meters.

Companies like Zoo Med make reptile carpet products that are packaged according to the size aquarium they will fill. For instance, enough carpet for a 55-gallon tank / 208 liters costs $7.94 / £4.70.

It's safe to say that if you budget $10 - $20 (£6.50 / £13) per month for substrate, you will be able to use the material of your choice (and that of your lizards) affordably.

d.) Veterinary Care

Like any pet, Frilled Lizards require some level of routine veterinary care in order to remain healthy. Unfortunately, not all veterinarians have expertise or experience in dealing with reptiles so you may need to spend a little more on your vet visits than you would for a cat or dog.

A general visit may cost between $40 and $80 (£26 to £52), but you should only need one visit per year. This averages to a budgeted cost of about $5 (£3.25) per month. Keep in mind that any tests or treatments performed during the visit will cost extra.

An even more pressing concern, however, is finding an exotic veterinarian who has experience treating reptiles. You can start your search at the official website for

The Association of Reptilian and Amphibian Veterinarians at www.arav.org in the United States. In the United Kingdom, consult www.reptilevets.co.uk.

e.) Habitat Repairs/Replacements

Over time, you are likely to need to make repairs and replacements in your Frilled Lizard's enclosure. These costs may include, but are not limited to:

- replacing damaged decorations
- repairing cracks or chips in the glass or Plexiglas
- purchasing bulbs for the lamps
- replacing a defective heating mat

These costs will vary, but you should budget about $10 (£6.50) per month to be safe. (Any single expense may be more, so setting a little money aside is a good idea.)

f.) Summary of Monthly Costs

Cost Type	One Lizard	Two Lizards
Food (insects)	$30 to $50 (£19.50 to £32.50)	$60 to $100 (£39 to £65)
Supplements	$15-$20 (£9.75-£13)	$30-$40 (£19.50-£26)
Substrate	$10-$20 (£6.50-£13)	$20-$40 (£13-£26)
Veterinary Care	$5 (£3.25)	$10 (£6.50)
Repairs/Replacements	$10 (£6.50)	$10 (£6.50)
Total:	$70 to $105 (£45.50 to £62.13)	$140 to $200 (£82.84 to £118.34)

7.) Pros and Cons of Frilled Lizards

As is true of all pets, Frilled Lizards have their supposed pros and cons. Before you decide whether this pet is truly the right choice for you, take the time to learn both sides of the story.

Pro and con lists are always difficult, as what one person sees as a negative, another might perceive as a positive. Below I've put together an overview of how some of these factors seem to be typically regarded, but of course all such factors boil down to a matter of personal preference.

a.) Pros of Frilled Lizards

- Very active and entertaining to keep as pets
- Captive-bred specimens take well to handling and can be tamed with regular handling
- Do well in captivity provided adequate space and branches for climbing
- Diet is not difficult to provide for – mostly crickets and various worms typically fed to reptiles
- Can be bred at home with relatively little difficulty
- Very attractive and unique species of lizard
- Frequent handling from a young age will encourage interaction and bonding with the keeper

b.) Cons of Frilled Lizards

- Wild-caught specimens may be skittish and difficult to handle even with time and patience
- Require a significant amount of space – horizontal and vertical
- May be difficult to find a pre-built enclosure due to height requirements for the species
- Getting the hang of temperature and light regulation can take some time
- Grow to be fairly large – up to 3 feet (0.9 m) in length
- Lifespan is very long (about 20 years) – requires a long-term commitment
- Fairly territorial species – two males should not be housed together

Chapter 3 – Purchasing Frilled Lizards

Now that you are confident in your understanding of the Frilled Lizard and are sure it is the right pet for you, you can move on to thinking about where and how to purchase one as a pet.

In this chapter you will learn where you can buy Frilled Lizards and how to choose one that is healthy. After all, you do not want to go through the preparation process only to bring home a new pet and have it fall ill. The information in this chapter will help you to ensure a long and healthy life for your new pet.

1.) Where to Buy Frilled Lizards

When it comes to finding a Frilled Neck Lizard for sale, you need to be careful (and somewhat particular) about where you acquire your pet.

You may be able to find this species at your local pet store, but this might not be the best option. Below you will find recommendations for purchasing Frilled Lizards in both the U.S. and the UK.

a.) Buying in the U.S.

In the United States it is a fairly good possibility that you can find a Frill Neck Lizard for sale in a local pet store, provided you live in a reasonably large urban area. The thing you need to think about, however, is where the pet store gets their lizards. If the store can't or won't tell you, this may be a "deal breaker."

If the pet store buys the lizards they offer for sale from a questionable source, the animals may already be suffering from disease or stress.

If you plan to purchase from a pet store, be prepared to ask some questions and to walk out if you don't get answers you like, or any answers at all.

In particular, you want to know if the lizards are wild caught or captive bred, and if they are captive bred, the name and location of the breeder. In some instances, breeders will sell only to stores, but in others, you can contact the operation directly about buying a pet.

Since stores don't always provide the correct environment for animals like Frilled Lizards, it's always best to go directly to a breeder if this option is available to you.

An excellent option in purchasing Frilled Lizards is to speak to local breeders or to attend a reptile show. Reptile shows provide herpetologists in the area with an opportunity to showcase and sell their animals.

Even if you do not buy your Frilled Lizard at such a venue, you can make connections with several breeders in your area and get their contact information. You should then be able to visit one or more of the establishments, see their lizards, ask questions, and make a more informed decision about your ultimate purchase.

Another option you might want to think about in purchasing or adopting a Frilled Lizard from a rescue organization. Reptile rescue groups routinely take in snakes, lizards and turtles that have been abandoned by their owners.

The benefit of adopting a rescue animal is that the lizard may already be tamed and used to handling. There is, however, also the risk that the animal will have been so neglected, that it has very little if any socialization.

This doesn't mean you can't tame the lizard with patience and kindness, but it will take longer and be more difficult. Without question, however, you will be performing a real service to take in an abandoned animal.

b.) Buying in the U.K.

Buying a Frilled Lizard in the UK is not significantly different from purchasing one in the U.S. You have the same options – buy from a local pet store, purchase from a reptile show or breeder, or find a local reptile rescue.

Do your research before you buy to find the most reputable source and the best price. Think carefully because where you get your Frilled Lizard could have a significant impact on its health and its likelihood of survival.

Note: Buying Frilled Lizards online may be tempting for the convenience of the transaction and the often-lower price. You have to consider, however, the fact that you do not know where the animal is coming from and that a living creature will be subject to the stress of transport before it reaches your home.

Many people consider the practice of shipping live animals to be cruel t because they may be exposed to extreme conditions and rough handling during the shipping process.

Please think carefully before purchasing a Frilled Lizard online and ensure that all care is taken to safeguard the animal in transit. Under ideal circumstances, if you do buy from an online breeder, you will be able to drive to the location and bring your new pet home yourself.

2.) How to Select a Healthy Frilled Lizard

Your first step in selecting a healthy Frilled Lizard is to determine whether the lizard you are looking at is captive-bred or wild-caught.

This can be difficult information to obtain, and if the store doesn't know or won't tell you, and the breeder is not forthcoming, you will likely want to move on to another purchase option.

a.) Wild Caught vs. Captive Bred

Wild-caught specimens tend to be more difficult to tame and they can also have a higher risk for carrying disease.

These lizards may also be suffering from the stress of capture and transport.

Captive-bred specimens are already used to living in the company of a keeper and they will likely be accustomed to being handled by humans.

b.) Physical Examination

Once you have determined that the Frilled Lizard was captive-bred, you can begin to examine the lizard to make sure it is healthy.

Condition of the Body

Start by looking at the overall condition of the body. A healthy lizard should look well fed, neither obese nor emaciated. If you can see the hip bones or the bones in the tail, it could be a sign of improper feeding.

Condition of the Skin

Check the skin of the lizard as well. If it is excessively wrinkled or dull, it could be a sign of dehydration. You should also make sure that the texture and tone of the skin is uniform with no signs of discoloration, bruising or bleeding visible.

Condition of the Orifices

Next, examine the orifices for signs of health and cleanliness. The eyes should be clear and free of discharge while the vent (the area under the tail) is free from caked feces.

The nose should also be clean and free from runny discharge, though some salty deposits are considered normal.

Condition of the Enclosure

You may also want to check the enclosure for signs of diarrhea. If you see a lot of messy fecal matter, it could be an indication that the animal is not properly cared for or that it is suffering from a health problem.

If you are looking at lizards in a fairly large breeding operation, make sure that all of the lizards are housed appropriately and have adequate space.

The Lizard's Behavior

In addition to examining the physical characteristics of the lizard, watch its behavior. A healthy Frilled Lizard will be active and alert, not hiding in a corner or moving with difficulty.

If you have an opportunity to hold the lizard you will be able to see for yourself how tame it is. Even well socialized lizards should be responsive and alert, but they will be more amenable and calm to handling than their wild caught counterparts.

If the lizard is slow or lethargic, it could be a sign of illness or simply that it is being kept in an environment that is too cool. In either case, it is likely to be stressed and/or ill as a result of improper conditions.

If you determine that the Frilled Lizard you are looking at is indeed healthy, you should have no qualms about bringing it home. Just make sure that you already have your lizard's habitat ready so the animal can immediately be placed in its new home.

Chapter 4 – Caring for You Frilled Lizard

Keeping a Frilled Lizard is just like keeping any other kind of pet – you are responsible for providing all the care your pet needs. For Frilled Lizards, these needs include proper housing and a healthy diet.

Frilled lizards should always be kept indoors in a heated tank and fed an insect-based diet. In this chapter you will learn everything you need to know about caring for your Frilled Lizard.

1.) Habitat Requirements

Your Frilled Lizard's habitat will most likely consist of a glass or Plexiglass enclosure decorated with wooden branches and heated with lamps and heating pads. Because these lizards come from a hot natural environment, temperature and lighting will be very important.

a.) Cage Size and Material

The size of enclosure you need depends on the size and age of your Frilled Lizard. While your lizard is small he may not need as much space as an adult.

Of course, to save yourself the hassle and cost of buying two separate enclosures over the lifetime of your lizard, you might be better off buying a larger cage in the beginning.

Juvenile Frilled Lizards can be kept in a tank between 20 and 40 gallons (75 to 151 liters) in capacity. For adult Frilled Lizards, however, the minimum tank dimensions are 4' x 3' x 6' (1.2 x 0.9 x 1.82 meters.)

It may seem strange to you that the recommended dimensions for a Frilled Lizard cage include a height that is greater than the width of the tank. Don't underestimate how active these lizards really are! They have a body perfectly designed for climbing.

In order to give your lizard the space he needs to move around and do what comes naturally to him, you will have to decorate the cage with plenty of wooden structures and branches. Giving your lizard adequate space will prevent him from developing abrasions and sores from bumping into the tank walls, and from just being bored and overly confined.

The ideal material for a Frilled Lizard tank is glass, although some owners do opt for Plexiglass. This is not my preference because it scratches easily and does not offer the same heat retaining ability as glass.

Since temperature maintenance is so crucial in Frilled Lizard husbandry, the slightly higher cost of glass is well worth the long-term benefits, plus it is easier to keep clean for maximum visibility.

The tank can be lined with recycled paper substrate or with reptile carpeting. Both of these options are affordable and fairly easy to clean. If you want to give your cage a more natural look, however, you can use Cyprus mulch.

Note: Although some enthusiasts do use play sand as a substrate, I don't recommend this choice. Frilled Lizards can accidentally ingest the sand while feeding, which can lead to potential gastrointestinal impaction. This condition can prove to be fatal.

b.) Heating and Lighting

Frilled Lizards are native to Australia and Indonesia where the temperatures are fairly high. In order to thrive properly in captivity, these conditions must be replicated in the home tank.

These lizards require two different temperature ranges within the tank – a hot side and a cool side. The temperature on the hot side of the tank should be between 95 and 102°F (35 to 39°C) while the cool side should be around 75 to 80°F (23 to 26°C).

In order to accomplish these temperatures you will need to install a number of heat lamps above your enclosure. The larger your lizard's cage, the more variation you will be able to achieve in tank temperature.

For the hotter area of the tank, provide a basking surface such as a flat rock or a strategically placed branch where your Frilled Lizard can rest in the heat. For cooler areas, give your lizard a place to hide and rest.

In colder weather or climates, you may also want to utilize heating pads or heating panels to keep the temperature in your lizard's tank within the proper range. These are typically placed under the enclosure.

In addition to heating, you also need to think about lighting, which is a health precaution as well as a matter of aesthetics.

Frilled Lizards are diurnal, which means that they are active and tend to feed during the day. To help activate their absorption of vitamins A and D, you will need to incorporate some UVB lighting in their tank.

Ideally, you should provide your lizard with 10 to 12 hours of 5.0 to 10.0 UVB light per day. You can accomplish this by using a combination UVB heat bulb or separate bulbs for heat and UVB.

2.) Feeding Frilled Lizards

Without a healthy diet, your lizards may fail to thrive and could be more at-risk for developing certain diseases. In this section you will learn the nutritional basics and receive tips for meeting them.

a.) Nutritional Needs

Frilled Lizards are carnivores. They receive the bulk of their daily nutritious from meat-based sources, generally insects like crickets, mealworms and the occasional mouse.

In the wild, they may also feed on small birds and snakes as well as other lizards. In captivity, the rule is variety – the greater variety you can provide your lizard in his diet, the healthier he will be.

In terms of actual nutritional requirements, there are a few things you need to know. Calcium is extremely important, but lizards that are fed only crickets are typically deficient. Crickets are a good source of protein, but not of calcium.

In order for your lizard to actual metabolize the calcium he ingests, he also needs plenty of vitamins A, D, E and the mineral phosphorus.

Because captive Frilled Lizards subsist on a diet that consists mainly of crickets, worms and other insects, you will need to supplement their meals with multi-vitamin and calcium powder dusted on the insects once or twice a week.

Another great option is to "gut-load" your feeder insects by feeding them healthy vegetables and fruits so the nutrients will be passed on to your lizard.

b.) Types of Food

Crickets should not comprise more than 50% of your lizard's diet. The other 50% should be made up of a variety of worms and other insects such as mealworms, wax worms, silk worms, super worms and earthworms.

Most of these insects can be purchased directly from your local pet store or ordered in bulk online.

Crickets and silk worms are an excellent source of protein. Wax worms are high in fat, which is good in small amounts only. Mealworms are very easy to come by, and you can even raise them yourself at home.

Many Frilled Lizard owners also recommend cockroaches, just be sure to pick a species that doesn't climb smooth surfaces or fly. If you do, you'll have lots of escapees and you'll have to live with them!

You can offer your Frilled Lizard mice, but only as an occasional treat. (Juvenile lizards should not be given mice because they are too large for them to properly digest. Adults, however, are capable of eating pinkie mice (newborns) and even mice as much as 3 to 4 weeks old.

If you live in an area where small lizards like house geckos are common, your Frilled Lizard may eat them as well. Just be sure to have your lizard examined by a vet regularly to make sure he isn't contracting parasites from the wild prey.

c.) Amount to Feed

The amount you need to feed your Frilled Lizard will vary depending on its age and appetite. While your lizard is a juvenile, feed him every other day as much as he will eat.

When he becomes an adult, reduce his feedings to two times per week. Generally, you can feed your lizard until he is full. Start by offering 3 to 5 crickets or worms. If the lizard eats them quickly, offer a few more and continue to do so until he stops eating.

Doing this will help you to get an idea of your lizard's appetite so you will be more likely to notice changes if they occur.

Once your lizard stops showing interest in food, stop feeding him. If you leave the insects in the cage they could burrow into the substrate and become a nuisance.

Chapter 5 - Breeding Frilled Lizards

Breeding reptiles is very different from breeding traditional pets like cats and dogs. It's not a task you should undertake lightly.

Though the process of breeding Frilled Lizards is very different from what you might expect, that is not to say it is impossible.

In fact, if you take the time to collect a healthy breeding pair and do your research to set up the proper environment, breeding Frilled Lizards is not especially difficult.

The first thing you need to think about when making the decision to breed your Frilled Lizards is your motivation for doing so. You may be tempted to breed your pets out of the desire to make some extra money selling the young.

In reality, it is very unlikely that you will make a profit at all. Breeding and raising Frilled Lizards takes a lot of time and money so it is something you should consider carefully before forging ahead.

In addition to thinking about your motivations for breeding, you also need to think about whether you can truly handle the additional costs and time requirements. Before you make your decision, take some of these factors into consideration:

- Do you have a compatible breeding pair or are you able to get one?
- Do you have time to devote to preparing your breeding pair for mating?

- Do you have the funds needed to feed and care for multiple Frilled Lizards?

- Do you have the experience or support of a veterinarian if something should go wrong?

- What are you going to do with the babies when they are ready to leave their parents?

- Do you have the space to keep multiple Frilled Lizards?

If none of these questions bring up any serious concerns, you may be ready to move on to learning about the process of breeding Frilled Lizards.

2.) Choosing a Breeding Pair

The first step in the breeding process for Frilled Lizards is, of course, to find a compatible breeding pair – one male and one female. Unfortunately, Frilled Lizards are very difficult to sex, so you may not be able to simply go to a pet store and pick out two lizards by sight.

Your best bet may be to start with a collection of young Frilled Lizards, raising them together until two of them naturally pair off. Another option is to contact a local breeder to purchase a pair that has already been sexed. If you do plan to pick out your own breeding pair, keep this information in mind:

- Female Frilled Lizards should be at least 2 years old before breeding. Younger females are more at-risk for egg binding (unable to pass an egg that has formed.)

- Male Frilled Lizards can be bred at one year of age.

- Males of the species are often a little larger with a slightly bigger head

- Females may be more skittish than males and may also exhibit duller coloration.

Once you have selected your breeding pair, you cannot simply jump into the mating process. Though it is not necessarily required, a two-month brumation period is recommended before Frilled Lizards are bred.

Brumation is the reptile equivalent of hibernation and it typically takes place during the winter months when food is less plentiful. For the best results, encourage your Frilled Lizard to enter brumation in November.

3.) Facilitating a Brumation Period

Before entering brumation, it is imperative that your Frilled Lizard's stomach be empty. During brumation, his body temperature will drop and bodily functions including digestion will slow down.

If he has food in his stomach, it could rot instead of being digested properly. Do not be alarmed if your lizard doesn't move much during brumation – this is completely natural.

To encourage brumation, reduce the temperatures in your Frilled Lizard's enclosure. Keep the daytime reading around 85 to 95° F (29 to 35° C) during the day and between 70 and 80 °F (21 to 27° C) at night.

You should also shorten the light cycle by about 2 hours. It is important that you make these temperature changes slowly over a period of several weeks. You may also want to separate males from females during this time.

As your Frilled Lizards prepare for brumation they will start to slow down. They will become less active and they will eat less as well.

Offer your lizards food every 7 to 10 days during brumation and increase the temperatures in the tank back to normal for 3 or 4 days to facilitate healthy digestion.

Your lizards may not eat every time you offer them food. If your pet refuses to eat, remove the food from the tank and keep the temperatures where they are. Maintain this routine for about 2 months until the spring.

To bring your lizards out of brumation, return the temperatures and lighting to normal levels. You do not have to make the transition as slowly as before, but instead alter the environment over the period of a week or so.

Do not feed your lizards until the temperature the lighting levels have come back to normal. At this time you can also begin misting your lizards' tank on a daily basis. This may help to encourage breeding.

4.) The Breeding Process

After your lizards have gone through the brumation period you will need to feed them to prepare them for breeding. Wait until your females look plump and well fed before introducing the male.

You may also want to supplement the female's diet with extra calcium to facilitate healthy egg production. Even before introducing the male and female lizards into the same tank, you may notice some breeding behavior such as head bobbing, extending of the frills, and stomping of the feet.

When your Frilled Lizards are ready for breeding, put the male and female together into the same habit and let them have undisturbed time. Observe your pets from a distance.

During mating, the female positions herself on the ground and the male aligns his vent with hers. In many cases, the male will bite the female's frill to keep her still. It is possible for female Frilled Lizards to store sperm, so a single mating could allow for fertile eggs for an entire breeding season.

Once fertilization has occurred, the female will enter a period of gestation in which the eggs develop inside her body. This period typically lasts about 45 days and you will be able to see the eggs growing inside her.

When the female is ready to lay her eggs you must provide a nest box, a large container filled with moist sand and soil where she can lay her eggs.

If you fail to provide a nest box, the female may refuse to lay the eggs and could become egg bound. Being unable to pass the eggs is a very dangerous and potentially fatal health condition.

The ideal dimensions for a nest box are 12" x 10" x 8" (30.5 x 25.4 x 20 cm). The substrate should be packed to a depth of about 6 inches (15 cm).

Female Frilled Lizards are capable of laying 2 to 4 clutches per season. The average clutch size is 6 to 8 eggs, though a range of 4 to 11 is common.

After the eggs have been laid, they must carefully be removed to an incubator and kept at a temperature between 82-84° F (27 to 29°C) until hatching.

A shallow plastic storage container with a hole cut in the top works very well as a "do it yourself" incubator. Fill the container about 1/3 full with incubation media (substrate.) A good choice is granular vermiculite

Collect the eggs and bury them halfway in the substrate and place the lid on top. Place the first container inside a foam cooler with a heating pad and monitor the temperature levels to a range of 82 to 84° F (27 to 28° C). Make sure the cooler also has a vent hole to allow steam to escape.

Never let the temperature in the incubator to go any higher than 86° F (30° C) or you will kill the embryos. With proper incubation, it typically takes 90 to 110 days for fertile eggs to hatch.

5.) Summary of Breeding Facts

- **Breeding Age**: 2 to 3 years average (minimum 2 years for females)
- **Prior to Breeding**: 2-month brumation period
- **Brumation Temperature**: daytime temperature 85 to 95° F (29 to 35° C), nighttime temperature 70 and 80° F (21 to 27° C)
- **Feeding**: every 7 to 10 days during brumation
- **Breeding Behavior**: head bobbing, extending the frills, and stomping the feet

- **Gestation Period**: average 45 days
- **Nest Box Dimensions**: 12" x 10" x 8", (30.5 x 25.4 x 20 cm)
- **Substrate**: moist sand and soil, depth of 6 inches (15 cm)
- **Average Clutch Size**: 6 to 8 average
- **Incubation**: between 82 and 84°F (27 to 29°C) until hatching
- **Hatching**: about 90 to 110 days

6.) Caring for the Babies

After a 90-110 day incubation period, the eggs will become indented, indicating they are ready to hatch. The baby lizards pierce the shells themselves and fight their way out of the eggs.

If some of the hatchlings appear to be struggling, do not fall prey to the temptation to help. It could take a while for the hatchlings to make it out of the shells, and they might have to stop for a rest. If you open the egg too soon, it could kill the hatchling.

Once the hatchlings have emerged, move them to a separate enclosure. Ideally, Frilled Lizard hatchlings should be raised individually but, if this is not possible, you can raise them in two or more small groups in separate cages.

Feed the hatchlings small pinhead crickets dusted with supplement powder twice a day until they are 4 to 5 months old. Make sure fresh water is available daily in a small dish and mist the tank with water several times a week to help with shedding as the hatchlings grow.

Chapter 6 - Keeping Frilled Lizards Healthy

As is true of all animals, Frilled Lizards are prone to experiencing certain health problems. Some are specifically linked to how the animal is being kept in captivity.

In order to keep your lizard healthy, you must understand how to identify and prevent these issues. In this chapter you will learn all you need to know about proactive healthcare for Frilled Lizards.

1.) Common Health Problems

Frilled Lizards are not especially prone to disease – at least, not any more than any other reptile – but they can fall ill from time to time. The key to keeping your lizard in optimal condition is to familiarize yourself with the most common health problems seen in this species.

Once you are aware of the potential problems you will be able to quickly identify them when they occur, make a diagnosis and begin the proper treatment. Some of the most common health problems seen in this species include:

- Bacterial Diseases
- Dysecdysis
- Fungal Dermatitis
- Limb Fractures
- Metabolic Bone Disease
- Mites
- Osteodystrophy
- Protein Deficiency
- Rostral Abrasions
- Septicemia

In the following pages you will find a detailed description of each of these conditions.

a.) Bacterial Diseases

Various bacterial diseases are fairly common in pet lizards. Those most typically seen manifest in the form of abscesses and granulomas.

An abscess is a swollen knot of tissue that is infected and contains an accumulation of pus, while a granuloma is also a formation of tissue, but generally without the pocket of pus. They are typically benign, but they can rupture, ulcerate, and cause swelling.

Abscesses on the limbs should be treated immediately because they could affect the underlying bone. Abscesses that occur internally may produce symptoms such as anorexia and vomiting.

Abscesses are generally diagnoses when a hard mass if felt underneath the skin, but part of the danger they present is that they can go undiagnosed for long periods, especially if they are internal.

b.) Dysecdysis

This condition occurs when the lizard does not properly shed its skin and may also be referred to as "retained shed." Dysecdysis may be caused by low humidity, ectoparasites, dermatitis, scars, or systemic disease.

If the skin doesn't properly shed, it can result in bacterial or fungal infections under the retained skin as well as loss of blood flow to the digits and eventual necrosis (rot.)

To prevent this condition, soak your lizard in lukewarm water for 10 minutes twice a week.

c.) Dermatitis

Either bacteria or fungi may cause dermatitis, or skin infections. These infections can occur anywhere on the body and, in many cases, spread rapidly. Necrotic dermatitis (skin rot) results in lesions and can lead to the loss of digits or limbs if not treated.

Another type of dermatitis, fungal dermatitis, occurs when the enclosure is too humid and wet. This condition typically manifests on the edges of the frill in the form of discolorations.

Treatment for dermatitis often involves cleaning of the area and treatment with antibiotics or antifungal medications.

d.) Limb Fractures

Limb fractures are not necessarily a disease, but they are a condition that Frilled Lizards can develop if not properly handled. Fractures can result from falls during jumping, fighting with cage mates, and improper handling.

Limb fractures are more likely to occur in lizards already suffering from nutritional osteodystrophy (defective bone development) or other nutritional deficiencies. If not properly treated, fractures can lead to lameness.

e.) Metabolic Bone Disease

Metabolic bone disease is a common result of nutritional deficiencies. It is most common in young lizards whose diets are low in calcium and vitamin D and in those that do not receive adequate exposure to natural sunlight or UVB light.

Some of the clinical signs of this condition include fractures and swelling in the legs, paralysis, weakness and, eventually, death. The best treatment for this condition is calcium supplementation and exposure to natural sunlight and UVB light.

f.) Mites

Infestations of mites are most likely to occur when the enclosure is overcrowded or unkempt. Heavy infestations can become very serious, leading to anemia and even death.

Symptoms of mites may include irritation and rubbing, roughened skin, and visible mite activity on the skin.

To test for mites, brush the lizard's body over a sheet of white fabric and examine the fabric closely for mites. There are several treatments for this condition including treatment with Ivermectin, Fenbendazole or Mebendazole.

g.) Osteodystrophy

Also known as nutritional oxteodystrophy, this condition is the result of calcium deficiency. Osteodystrophy is most common in juveniles, particularly when the diet is comprised primarily of crickets and roaches.

Osteodystrophy can be exacerbated by vitamin D deficiency resulting from inadequate exposure to U.V. light.

Osteodystrophy can lead to decalcification of bones and, eventually, deformities and bone fractures. To prevent this condition it is necessary to feed a variety of insects and to use calcium supplement powder once or twice a week.

h.) Protein Deficiency

Protein deficiency is the result of an inadequate diet – either too much of the same insect or feeding the wrong type of food.

This condition may also occur if the lizard stops eating due to environmental stress or disease. Some clinical signs of this condition include emaciation, depression, lethargy, and muscle atrophy.

i.) Rostral Abrasions

When your Frilled Lizard is kept in a cage that is too small, he may be prone to developing rostral abrasions – bumps and bruises from bumping into the tank walls. With repeated bumps, these abrasions may turn into sores, which can become painful and might inhibit the lizard's ability to eat normally.

These abrasions can also become infected, which could lead to malformation of the jaw. In the vent of infection, or obvious physical or functional impairment, the abrasions will require veterinary treatment.

j.) Septicemia

Septicemia is commonly caused by Gram-negative bacilli, usually *Aeromonas* and *Pseudomonas spp.* in Frilled Lizards. It is often concurrent with a localized infection and may be contracted via infection of a skin wound. This condition can also be transmitted by mites and is often precipitated by stress.

Some of the clinical signs and symptoms of Septicemia include sudden death, lethargy with decreased muscle tone and red coloration under the scales.

The infection is very serious and often proves fatal within 24 hours of onset. Antibiotics may be administered as a treatment, as well as fluid and vitamin therapy.

2.) Preventing Illness

In addition to familiarizing yourself with common health problems, routine daily health checks can help to prevent serious problems from developing. In this section you will learn the basics of preventing illness in your Frilled Lizard.

a.) Daily Health Checks

Every day you should spend a few minutes observing and examining your Frilled Lizard. It may seem silly to do this daily, but it is essential if you want to detect the presence of diseases early enough for prompt and proper treatment. This is the best chance your lizard has to make a full and quick recovery. Some of the things to look for include:

- Abnormal growths or swelling
- Change in posture or behavior
- Bleeding or discharge
- Skin irritation, discoloration or laceration
- Difficulty breathing
- Change in feces
- Convulsions or seizures
- Dehydration (loss of skin elasticity, sunken eyes)
- Abnormal shedding
- Vomiting
- Unusual activity level (hyperactive or lethargic)

- Abrasions on the nose or face
- Evidence of diarrhea

b.) Environment Checks

Also check the condition and quality of your lizard's environment on a daily basis. In particular, you want to ensure that the temperature, humidity and other parameters in the tank are stable and within the proper range. Some things to look for include:

- Temperature outside recommended range
- Inadequate food or water supply
- Lack of feces in the enclosure
- Excessive soiling
- Unusual odors
- Extreme humidity (or lack thereof)

- Broken enclosure or decorations
- Inadequate lighting or burnt out bulbs

For any animal kept in an enclosure, the number one consideration on the part of the keeper is cleanliness! The better you do your housekeeping chores on behalf of your lizard, the healthier your pet will be!

c.) Detailed Examination

If you suspect that your Frilled Lizard is suffering from a health problem, your first step should be to perform a physical examination. The purpose of this examination is to isolate and identify the problem to the best of your ability so you can effectively seek veterinary treatment.

Even when your lizard is not sick, it is a good idea to perform this kind of examination once in a while so both you and your pet get into the habit. The steps of a thorough physical examination are as follows:

1. Check for signs of normal breathing. The lizard shouldn't make a hissing or clicking noise when breathing.

2. Check the nose for signs of abrasions or infection including discharge and discoloration.

3. Examine the mouth for signs of swelling or scabbing. A slight yellow tinge is normal, but the gums should not be red.

4. Check the eyes. They should be clear and free of discharge. The expression should be bright, and the eyes should be responsive to light.

5. Examine the body. It should be free of lacerations and swelling and there should be no palpable or visible lumps or bumps.

6. Check the color of the lizard. It should be within the normal range without discoloration or redness.

7. Observe the lizard's condition. The tail bones and hip bones should not be protruding.

8. Check for bumps on the feet and legs. There should be none present and no swelling of any area including the joints.

9. Examine the cloaca (the area under the tail, also known as the vent.) It should be relatively clean and free of fecal matter, not swollen or inflamed.

10. Look at the tail. It should be free of lesions and swelling.

Note: If you discover evidence that may be a sign of disease, seek veterinary care for your Frilled Lizard as soon as possible. The sooner you seek care, the sooner your lizard can get the treatment he needs.

If you are living in an area where you do not have ready access to an exotic veterinarian, seek the assistance of more experienced lizard keepers, even to the extent of asking for advice in online enthusiast communities.

Although increasingly popular as pets, Frilled Lizards are still sufficiently rare that owners are an invaluable resource for one another. A good place to begin is The Frilled Dragon Forum at www.thefrilleddragon.com.

Please refer to the resource links at the end of this book for more links to useful information.

3.) Human Health Concerns

Any time a reptile or an amphibian is kept as a pet, there is the potential for its human caregivers to contract salmonella.

The U.S. Centers for Disease Control recommended in March 2012 that neither amphibians nor reptiles should be present in homes where children of less than 5 years of age are also resident, or in homes with people who have a compromised immune system.

In almost all cases, so long as the creature's habitat is correctly maintained, disease transmission to humans won't be a problem, but there are some "best practices" I want to mention.

Before and after you handle your pet, give it food, or clean its habitat, WASH YOUR HANDS. Also, don't keep your pet close to any area where food is being prepared.

---

a.) What is Salmonella?

The illness salmonella or salmonellosis affects the human intestinal tract. It is similar to, but not synonymous with food poisoning. These are two unique and separate conditions.

A bacterium causes salmonella, and it is from the same group of bacteria that causes:

- food poisoning
- gastroenteritis
- enteric fever
- typhoid fever

The most common salmonella symptom is severe diarrhea, but a sufferer may also experience:

- abdominal cramps
- blood in the stool
- fever and chills
- headache
- muscle pains
- nausea and vomiting

Whatever symptoms you do have will last from one week to ten days and in most cases resolve on their own. The most important thing is to drink lots of water so you stay hydrated.

If your doctor thinks that the bacteria has gotten into your bloodstream, you may have to take a course of antibiotics. Even if diarrhea is present, you shouldn't use antimotility drugs to stop it. Your system has to fight the pathogen and expel all the bacteria from your body.

The sooner it's gone, the faster you'll get better! If you use drugs to stop the diarrhea, you will lengthen the duration of your illness.

b.) How is Salmonella Transmitted?

Humans typically get salmonella from one of the following sources:

- seafood and poultry that is raw or under-cooked
- raw eggs and recipes that call for them (mayonnaise)
- fruits and vegetables that have not been washed
- produce washed in contaminated water
- food prepared in dirty kitchens
- failure to wash hands before/after handling food
- pet reptiles and amphibians

Although they, themselves, are immune to infection, many reptiles and amphibians do have salmonella present in their guts and shed the bacteria in their feces. Anything that comes into contact with the droppings, or with the animal's skin is exposed to the bacteria.

c.) Argument Against Reptilian Pets?

The potential risk of contracting salmonella should not be taken as an argument against having pet reptiles. Cat lovers have hardly given up their companions for fear of cat scratch fever, nor have dedicated dog lovers sent Fido away due to the chance of a tick borne illness like Lyme's Disease.

The key to keeping yourself safe from infection with a pet reptile is scrupulous husbandry of the animal's habit paired with washing your hands BEFORE and AFTER interacting with your pet. Do those simple things, and you should be able to safely enjoy having a pet reptile in your home.

Chapter 7 - Frilled Lizards Care Sheet

Having made it this far through the book, you may feel overwhelmed by the sheer volume of information you have obtained. There will be times when you need to find a quick answer to a question, but you do not want to flip through the entire book to find it.

In this chapter you will find a summary of facts from all the key components of caring for a Frilled Lizard – basic information, habitat, feeding/nutrition and breeding. You will also find bonus information about cleaning your lizard's cage and more.

1.) Basic Information

Scientific Classification: *Chlamydosaurus kingii*
Other Names: frill neck lizard, frilled dragon, King's lizard

Native Environment: northern Australia and southern New Guinea

Natural Habitat: humid climates, forests and savannahs

Size: grows up to 3 feet (0.9 m) in length

Temperament: can be tamed with frequent handling from a young age

Lifespan: about 20 years

Other Pets: should not be kept with other lizards

Diet: primarily insectivorous in captivity

Reproduction: breed during the spring after 2-month period of brumation (hibernation)

Average Clutch Size: 6 to 8, can be up to 11 eggs

2.) Habitat Set-up Guide

Natural Habitat: northern Australia, southern New Guinea

Native Environment: tropical savannah, humid climates

Habits: arboreal (lives in trees)

Minimum Cage Dimensions: 4' x 3' x 6' (1.2 x 0.9 x 1.82 meters)

Decorations: wooden structures and branches

Substrate: recycled paper substrate or reptile carpeting; Cyprus mulch for authentic look

Material: glass is ideal

Tank Environment: hot side and cool side

Tank Temperature: hot side between 95 and 102° F (35 to 39° C), cool side around 75 to 80° F (23 to 26° C)

Lighting: 10 to 12 hours of 5.0 to 10.0 UVB light per day

3.) Feeding/Nutrition Info

Dietary Habits: carnivorous in the wild, insectivorous in captivity

Primary Nutritional Needs: calcium, Vitamins A, D and E, phosphorus

Foods to Offer: crickets, mealworms, earthworms, silk worms, wax worms, super worms, pinkie mice

Supplements: calcium and multi-vitamin several times per week

Recommendations: gut-load feeder insects

Amount to Feed: as much as he will eat

Feeding Frequency: juveniles every other day, adults twice per week

4.) Breeding Facts

Breeding Age: 2 to 3 years average (minimum 2 years for females)

Prior to Breeding: 2-month brumation (hibernatnion) period

Brumation Temperature: daytime temperature in a range of 85 to 95° F (29 to 35° C), nighttime temperature from 70 to 80°F (21 to 27° C)

Feeding: every 7 to 10 days during brumation (hibernation)

Breeding Behavior: head bobbing, extending the frills and stomping the arms and feet

Gestation Period: average 45 days

Nest Box Dimensions: 12″ x 10″ x 8″, (30.5 x 25.4 x 20 cm)

Substrate: moist sand and soil, depth of 6 inches

Average Clutch Size: 6 to 8 average

Incubation: between 82 and 84°F (27 to 29°C)

Hatching: about 90 to 110 days

5.) Cleaning the Enclosure

Part of keeping your Frilled Lizard happy and healthy involves keeping the enclosure clean. Let's face it, your pet isn't going to clean his own house, so that responsibility falls completely to you!

On a daily basis, refresh your lizard's water supply. Many lizards do their "business" in their water bowls so you will want to clean the receptacles frequently to avoid contamination from urine and feces.

You should also spot-clean the tank, removing feces and any bits of debris, especially uneaten food. It is generally not necessary to remove the lizard from the tank to perform these daily chores.

When it comes to large-scale cleaning, however, you should remove your lizard to a safe location. Once a week, remove all of the décor and other items from the tank including the substrate.

Check your local pet store for a reptile-safe disinfectant that you can use on the walls and floor of the tank. Avoid household cleaners because they may contain chemicals that are dangerous for your lizard.

Clean the dishes and tank decorations in warm water and let them dry before placing them back in the tank. Once the tank is reassembled, you can return your lizard to his home.

Chapter 8 – Common New Owner Mistakes

When you first bring your Frilled Lizard home, you are likely to go through a learning period that can be a little scary and even intimidating. It's one thing to read about caring for these animals and another thing entirely to do it yourself!

Don't worry. It's common for new owners to make a few mistakes. By reading this chapter, however, you can familiarize yourself with some of the most serious "goofs" and avoid them altogether.

1.) Breeding Too Early

The recommended breeding age for Frilled Lizards is between 2 and 3 years of age. Though males of the species can be bred at one year, this can be very dangerous for females due to their small build, which can lead to birthing complications like egg binding.

It is also important to consider the fact that egg production requires a great deal of calcium, which can deprive a female of this essential nutrient if she is still growing and developing. For the overall health and safety of your Frilled Lizards, wait until they are at least 2 years old to breed them.

2.) Improper Cage Temperature

Frilled Lizards are ectothermic creatures, which means that they rely on their environment to regulate their bodily temperature. If it drops too low, the lizard will not be able to digest food properly and could experience a number of other complications.

Ideally, your tank should provide a range of temperatures both hot and cool. The hot side should range between 95 and 102° F (35 to 39° C) while the cool side should be around 75 to 80° F (23 to 26° C.)

In order to accomplish this you will need to install a combination of heat lamps and heating pads and provide your lizard with a basic spot, typically a large, flat stone where you pet can really soak up the heat.

3.) Lack of Proper Diet

In order to keep your Frilled Lizard happy and healthy you need to understand and provide for his dietary needs. Frilled Lizards are carnivorous in the wild but, in captivity, tend to eat an insect-based diet.

From maximum nutrition, offer your pet a wide variety of insects including crickets, mealworms, wax worms, silk worms, earthworms and even the occasional pinkie mouse.

Many new lizard owners make the mistake of feeding their lizard too many crickets, which are a good source of protein but lack calcium and other vital nutrients.

To fill the nutritional gaps in your lizard's diet, dust the feeder insects with calcium or multi-vitamin supplements once or twice a week.

4.) Cage is Too Small

Frilled Lizards can grow up to 3 feet (0.9 meters) in length, but they start off fairly small. As a pet owner, you need to decide whether to buy one cage for when your lizard is young and get a larger cage when it grows up.

Unfortunately, many new owners make the mistake of purchasing a smaller cage for their juvenile lizard and never upgrading the tank once he grows. Having a cage that is too small can cause a number of problems for Frilled Lizards.

Not only may they fail to grow and thrive properly, but they could also suffer from bumps and abrasions from running into the tank walls. For an adult Frilled Lizard, the minimum cage dimensions recommended are 4′ x 3′ x 6′ (1.2 x 0.9 x 1.82 meters.)

5.) Keeping with Other Lizards

Inexperienced Frilled Lizard owners often wonder if these lizards can be kept with other species as long as the habitat requirements are similar. This question is most commonly directed toward bearded dragons, another species of Australian lizard.

The reality is that Frilled Lizards do not generally get along with other lizards. In fact, they may regard smaller species as prey. For the best results, keep only female Frilled Lizards together or one male with one or more females.

Two males, when housed together, will almost always fight, displaying often bloody, and even fatal, territorial aggression toward one another. Two Frilled Lizard males fighting is a vicious sight with significant consequences, and never a situation you want to facilitate in any way!

Chapter 9 – Frequently Asked Questions

Even after reading this book you may have questions about the care and keeping of Frilled Lizards. While it is impossible to answer every question out there, hopefully you will have found the information you need within the pages of this book.

For further reference and as a "quick start," for those readers who tend to turn to the back of the book first, here are some answers to frequently asked questions about housing, feeding, breeding, health care and more.

Q: How big do Frilled Lizards get?

A: The average size for a full-grown adult Frilled Lizard is about 3 feet (0.9 m) from nose to tail. Females of the species may be slightly smaller than males, however.

Q: Do I have to build my own Frilled Lizard cage?

A: Many Frilled Lizard owners choose to build their own cages so they can customize the size and dimensions. Keep in mind that Frilled Lizards are arboreal lizards so they like to spend their time in trees.

This being the case, you will need a cage that is tall as well as wide. Premade cages with these dimensions are often very expensive so it might be more economical to build your own. If you're not a "do it yourself" type, you can generally find someone to help you with the project.

Q: Is my Frilled Lizard captive-bred or wild-caught?

A: The only way to find out is to ask. Before you buy, make sure you speak to the breeder to try to discover where the lizards come from and whether or not they are used to handling by humans.

If you are not able to speak to the breeder directly, you might take some clues from the lizard's behavior. If it is very skittish and fearful of humans, it could be a wild-caught specimen that hasn't been fully tamed.

Q: Why is the cage temperature important?

A: Frilled Lizards, like most reptiles, are ectothermic. They rely on the temperature of the environment around them to regulate their body temperature.

Unlike humans, lizards do not have a set body temperature and, if their body temperature drops too low, it could inhibit vital functions such as digestion.

In order to keep your lizard's body running as it should you need to maintain a proper temperature in your lizard's tank.

Ideally, their habitat should have a hot and cool side. The hot side should be kept at 95 and 102° F (35 to 39° C) while the cool side should be around 75 to 80° F (23 to 26° C.)

Q: What do I do if my Frilled Lizard stops eating?

A: Frilled Lizards are notorious for going through random bouts of anorexia – periods during which they inexplicably stop eating. While this is a common behavior, it is still a good idea to get him checked out by a veterinarian to make sure there are no underlying medical causes for his lack of appetite. Your vet may also be able to make suggestions for how to get him to start eating again.

Q: Are Frilled Lizards a good choice for beginners?

A: If you have never owned a reptile before, you may not want to start out with a Frilled Lizard. These lizards have very specific requirements in terms of habitat and environment, which can be difficult for a novice.

It is not that Frilled Lizards are dangerous or difficult to handle, they just require more specialized care than other species.

Q: Can I feed my Frilled Lizard vegetables?

A: Many lizards, particularly iguanas, actually require vegetation as part of their diet. Frilled Lizards, on the other hand, are insectivores and get most of their nutrition from insects.

There is no harm in offering your Frilled Lizard a small amount of vegetables, but there is no guarantee that he will eat them. Every lizard is different, however, so you won't know unless you try.

Q: Is it okay to breed my Frilled Lizards?

A: Breeding Frilled Lizards is not especially difficult but it is not something that the average owner should undertake without careful consideration.

It may seem like an exciting challenge but you also need to think about the time and monetary ramifications of breeding your lizards and what you are going to do with the babies.

If you are not looking to make a profit and have a way to provide the babies with suitable homes, you can certainly consider breeding your Frilled Lizards.

Q: Why is my Frilled Lizard's skin peeling off?

A: Shedding is normal and healthy for Frilled Lizards – for all reptiles, in fact. Each lizard may exhibit a slightly different pattern when it comes to shedding.

Some will start shedding on the head and extremities then shed the skin on the body while others may shed all of it at the same time.

Never pull shedding skin off your Frilled Lizard because it may not be ready to come off and you could damage the delicate skin underneath. The tattered skin may look uncomfortable to you, but it's not for the lizard.

To help your lizard with shedding, soak him in a lukewarm bath for 10 minutes or so two or three times a week.

Q: What kind of vitamins do Frilled Lizards need?

A: Calcium is incredibly important for Frilled Lizards but other nutrients such as Vitamins A and D are important as well. Deficiencies in these nutrients can lead to metabolic bone disease, kidney problems, and more.

To ensure your Frilled Lizard's health, dust his feeder insects with calcium or multi-vitamin supplement powder once or twice a week.

Q: Can I feed my Frilled Lizard mice?

A: The Frilled Lizard is largely insectivorous but they may eat the occasional pinkie mouse. It is important to wait until your lizard is large enough to accept this type of prey.

Do not offer mice more than once or twice a month. Start off with pinkie mice (newborns) and do not offer anything larger than a baby mouse that is 3 to 4 weeks old.

Feeder mice are easily obtained at large pet stores.

Q: Do I need to bathe my Frilled Lizard?

A: Frilled Lizards do not need a bath to keep clean, but they will benefit from soaking in lukewarm water for 10 minutes twice a week.

This loosens dead skin and aids your lizard in healthy shedding. Regular soaking will help to prevent conditions like dysecdysis, or "retained shed."

Q: Why is my lizard's nose swollen?

A: Swelling and abrasions on the nose are common in Frilled Lizards when they are kept in a cage that is too small. The lizard may bump into the walls or jump at them in an attempt to escape.

To prevent this, make sure your lizard's enclosure is large enough to accommodate him safely. If you begin with a small enclosure for a young or juvenile Frilled Neck, plan on expanding in the future.

Q: How do I incubate my lizard's eggs?

A: To create your own incubator you need to select a shallow plastic storage container with a hole cut in the top for ventilation. Fill the container about 1/3 full with incubation media then rinse the substrate until the water runs clear.

Collect the eggs and bury them halfway in the substrate and place the lid on top. Place the container in a foam cooler that has been heated to 82 to 84°F (27 to 28°C) using a heating pad. Make sure to create a vent hole in the lid of the cooler to allow steam to escape.

Q: What do Frilled Neck Lizards eat?

A: Frilled Lizards are likely to eat any insect you give them, but some are better nutritionally than others. Crickets are a staple of the Frilled Lizard diet but they shouldn't compose more than 50% of what your lizard eats.
Other insects your lizard is likely to enjoy include various roaches, earthworms, mealworms, silk worms, wax worms and super worms. Don't hesitate to try a variety!

Chapter 10 – Frilled Lizard Facts for Kids

- Frilled Lizards can get really big. They may grow as long as 3 feet (0.9 m).

- Frilled Lizards can be found in Australia and New Guinea.

- They can stand up on their hind legs and run at different speeds.

- Frill Neck Lizards spend 90% of their time in trees in the wild.

- Two-thirds of a Frilled Lizard's body length is taken up by his tail.

- Sometimes Frilled Lizards are confused with Bearded Dragons.

- Both male and female Frill Neck Lizards have the impressive flap of skin around their necks that they can extend into a big, pleated collar.

- Sometimes they put out their frills to frighten off something they see as a threat, but at other times, they're just trying to cool themselves off.

- These lizards are also called Frilled Dragons and they do look like strange creatures out of a storybook!

- In the wild, Frill Neck lizards are carnivores, they eat meat, but when they live as pets, they do very well on a diet of insects.

- The Frilled Neck Lizard was once pictured on the Australian two-cent coin.

- These lizards can live as long as 20 years!

- Frilled Neck Lizards can change color to blend in with their surroundings.

- Before a female Frill Necked Lizard has babies, she needs to sleep for two months. This is called "brumation."

- These lizards are not dangerous. They don't have any venom, and if they're handled from the time they're little, they're very friendly.

Chapter 11 – Relevant Websites

Though this book is packed full of information regarding the care and keeping of Frilled Lizards, you may find yourself wanting a few more resources.

Whether you are looking for information about feeding, habitat set-up or breeding, in the following pages you will find everything you need.

The collections of websites are from both U.S. and UK sources. Like all things online, however, I can make no guarantee that these websites will still be in place when you attempt to access them. All were active at the time of the writing of this book in mid-2014.

1.) Food for Frilled Lizards

These websites offer information about the nutritional needs of Frilled Lizards, the types of food that are best for them, and what kind of treats they enjoy.
United States Websites:

"Frilled Dragons."
LLLReptile.
lllreptile.com/info/library/animal-care-sheets/lizards-and-monitors/-/f+rilled-dragons/

"Frill-Necked Lizard."
BioExpedition.com.
bioexpeditioc+cn.com/frill-necked-lizard-frilled-lizard/
"Frilled Lizard."

Doctors Foster and Smith. +pic/article.cfm?aid=2495

United Kingdom Websites:

"Frilled Dragon."
Appleton Exotics.
www.appletonexotics.co.uk/frilled-dragon/

"Frilled Lizard Care Sheet."
Martin's Reptiles.
www.martinsreptiles.co.uk/frilliecare.htm

"Frilled Dragon (Chlamydosaurus kingii)."
The Living Rainforest.
 www.the-livingrainforest.co.uk/living/
view_caresheet.php?id=24

2.) Care for Frilled Lizards

These websites provide tips about creating the ideal Frilled Lizard habitat and suggest ways for keeping your pets happy in their captive homes. Remember that you can also search for habitat images to get innovative design ideas.

United States Websites:

"Frilled Lizard."
Stahl Exotic Animal Veterinary Services.
www.seavs.com/lizards/frilledlizard.html

"Australian Animals – Frilled Lizard."

Oracle ThinkQuest.
library.thinkquest.org/5053/Australia/australianfrilledlizard
.html

"Frilled Dragon Care Sheet."
FaunaClassifieds.com.
www.faunaclassifieds.com/forums/showthread.php?t=7774
2

United Kingdom Websites:

"Frilled Dragon Care Sheet."
Tyrannosaurus Pets.
www.tyrannosauruspets.co.uk/caresheets/45-care-
frilleddragon

"Frill Necked Lizard."
South Shields Lizards.
www.southshieldslizards.co.uk/factfiles/Lizards/FrillNecke
dLizard.php

"Frilled Dragon."
Reptile Cymru.
www.reptilecymru.co.uk/caresheets/Frilled%20dragon.pdf

3.) Health Info for Frilled Lizards

Here you will find information regarding keeping your
Frilled Lizards healthy including common illnesses seen in
this species.

United States Websites:

"Frilled Lizard."
Stahl Exotic Animal Veterinary Services.
www.seavs.com/lizards/frilledlizard.html

"Frilled Dragon Info."
RubixReptiles.com. www.rubixreptiles.com/home/Frilled-Dragon-Care/health

"Frilled Dragon Care."
AlamoCityAgama.
www.alamocityagama.com/frilleddragoncare

"Health."
TheFrilledDragon.com.
www.thefrilleddragon.com/archive/index.php/f-4.html

"Reptile Health Articles."
ReptileChannel.com.
www.reptilechannel.com/reptile-health/reptile-health-topiclist.aspx

United Kingdom Websites:

"Reptile Health, Reptile Care and Lizard Care."
Vetark.co.uk.
www.vetark.co.uk/pages/Health_3.aspx

"Reptile and Amphibian Healthcare."
CaptiveBredReptileForums.co.uk.
www.captivebredreptileforums.co.uk/general-reptile-amphibian/42788-reptile-amphibian-healthcare.html

4.) General Info for Frilled Lizards

These websites offer an overview of the species including the breed history, personality traits, and general info. The more you understand the natural history and environmental needs of your pets, the better you will be able to care for captive Frilled Neck Lizards. Plus, many of these sites have fascinating video content!

United States Websites:

"Frilled Lizard."
National Geographic.
animals.nationalgeographic.com/animals/reptiles/frilled-lizard/

"Frilled Lizard (Chlamydosaurus kingii)."
Arkive.org.
www.arkive.org/frilled-lizard/chlamydosaurus-kingii/

"Frilled Lizard."
American Museum of Natural History.
www.amnh.org/exhibitions/past-exhibitions/lizards-and-snakes-alive/sight-hounds/a-world-of-sights/frilled-lizard

"Frilled Neck Lizard."
AustralianFauna.com.
www.australianfauna.com/frillednecklizard.php

United Kingdom Websites:

"Frilled Lizard."
BBC.co.uk.
www.bbc.co.uk/nature/life/Frill-necked_Lizard

"Frilled Lizard."
Kidcyber.com.au.
www.kidcyber.com.au/topics/frilledliz.htm

"Frilled Neck Lizard."
Australian Reptile Park.
www.reptilepark.com.au/animalprofile.asp?id=84

5.) Breeding Frilled Lizards

In these websites you will find tips for choosing a breeding pair, preparing for the breeding process and raising the young.

United States Websites:

"Breeding Frilled Dragons."
TheFrilledDragon.com.
www.thefrilleddragon.com/content/126-Breeding-Frilled-Dragons

"Frilled Dragon Care Sheet."
Reptile and Exotics Protection Society.
www.reptileexoticprotectionsociety.com/frilledlizards.htm

"Breeding the Flamboyant Frilled Dragon."
ReptileChannel.com.
www.reptilechannel.com/
lizards/breeding-lizards/frilled-dragon-breeding.aspx

United Kingdom Websites:

"Frilled Lizard, Frillneck Lizard, King's Lizard."
BBC.co.uk.
www.bbc.co.uk/nature/wildfacts/factfiles/3041.shtml

"Frilled Lizard Care Sheet."
Martin's Reptiles.
www.martinsreptiles.co.uk/frilliecare.htm

"Frilled Dragon."
Wingham Wildlife Park.
winghamwildlifepark.co.uk/animal/frilled-dragon

Afterword

In this text, I've done my best to introduce you to the Australian Frilled Neck Lizard, one of the most visually unique of all captive exotic reptiles. With proper handling and socialization from an early age, a Frill Neck Lizards are congenial pets.

They do grow quite large; reaching an adult length of as much as 3 feet (0.9 m), so this is not a species you'll be tucking away in an aquarium in the living room. Also, since these lizards spend 90% of their in trees in the wild, they need a lot of vertical space when kept as pets.

As I have said, I don't recommend this species for children or for novice reptile keepers. Frill Necks have specific needs in terms of diet, temperature, and lighting that makes their husbandry precise if not difficult.

Obviously they are primarily prized for their bright, intelligent dispositions, but also for their distinctive appearance, especially when they extend the "frill" or cape of skin that hangs from their neck and around their shoulders.

When extended, the frill forms a circular pleated ruff that is usually very colorful. At the same time, the lizard will open his mouth to display the bright yellow flesh found inside, while hissing convincingly and menacingly. If he has enough room, a Frill Neck may then stand up on his hind legs and take off running.

This is, to say the very least, not your average lizard! For many people having one of these beauties as a pet is about as close as they will ever come to owning a real life dinosaur of a living equivalent of a dragon, which is why you will sometimes see this species called the "Frilled Dragon Lizard."

Although they are indeed descended from the dinosaurs, as are all reptiles and amphibians, you won't find your Frill Neck breathing fire in your living room or basement. In fact, in spite of his large size, this is a most convivial fellow. Since your Frill Neck can easily be with you for as long as 20 years, this good disposition is certainly one of the "pluses" of the species.

If you are not prepared to make a two-decade commitment to the welfare of a living animal, however, stop immediately. When a Frilled Lizard comes into your life, he will depend on you to meet all of his needs for food, water, and shelter.

If you can't do that, don't adopt a lizard or any other kind of pet. In making a decision to live with a companion animal, the emphasis is always on the welfare of the animal. You can take care of yourself. He or she is out of his element and completely dependent on your good graces for survival.

Having taken everything you've learned in this book into consideration, and weighing all the factors, make the right choice for yourself and the lizard. If that choice is to share a home, congratulations, you have likely just acquired the most unusual pet on your block – or maybe even in your entire town.

While companion reptiles are not interactive after the fashion of a dog or cat, they have distinct personalities in their own right. They are fascinating to watch, and offer rewarding challenges in husbandry and habitat design.

And you'll never tire of the shocked reaction the first time a new person looks at your pet and exclaims, "What the heck IS that?!"

Glossary

Ambient Temperature – The overall temperature of the environment in which your pet's habitat is placed, i.e. room temperature.

Amphibian - A vertebrate animal with cold blood that has lungs and is capable of living on water or land. Generally starts out life in the water and progresses to a terrestrial stage.

Arboreal – Animals that live primarily in trees or bushes. Frilled Neck lizards spend approximately 90% of their time off the ground clinging to tree trunks.

Brumation – The equivalent of hibernation in animals, a period of near comatose inactivity seen in reptiles, generally occurring during the winter.

Cloaca – A chamber opening through the anus used for both excretion and reproduction. It is located in an area under the tail referred to as the "vent."

Diurnal – Animals that are active and feeding during the day as opposed to those that are nocturnal, or active at night.

Ectothermic - An animal that is incapable of regulating its own body temperature, and relies on the ambient temperature of the surrounding environment to do so for him. When kept in captivity, such animals require artificial sources of heat.

Egg Binding – A dangerous condition that sometimes presents in Frilled Lizard females that prevents them from depositing their eggs. It can be fatal.

Frill – In Frilled Neck Lizards, the frill is a loose flap of skin around the neck that can be raised and extended into a large pleated "ruff." Used in communication and as a warning to predators.

Gut-Loading – The practice of feeding prey insects nutritious foods so the nutrients are passed on to the lizard, generally to enhance the amount of vitamins and minerals the reptile ingests.

Gravid – A female bearing embryos or eggs (pregnant.)

Herpetology – The branch of science that focuses on the study of both reptiles and amphibians. Often erroneously assumed to be the study of snakes only.

Oviparous – An animal that lays eggs, which later hatch thus accomplishing propagation of the species.

Reptile – Reptiles are vertebrates with cold blood and include snakes, lizards, crocodiles, turtles, and tortoises. They typically have dry scaly skin, and lay soft-shelled eggs on land.

Substrate - Any material used to form the "bed" of an aquarium or terrarium environment. The primary concern with Frilled Lizards is to choose a substance they will not eat, leading to intestinal impaction.

Terrarium – A terrarium is an enclosure, typically made of glass and sometimes Plexiglass in which reptiles and amphibians are kept as pets.

Vent – The accepted name for the anal region under the tail of birds, amphibians, and reptiles, which provides an opening on the outside of the body to the cloaca.

Works Cited

Alderton, David. *Firefly Encyclopedia of the Vivarium: Keeping Amphibians, Reptiles, and Insects, Spiders and other Invertebrates in Terraria, Aquaterraria, and Aquaria.* Firefly Books, 2007.

Bartlett, Richard and Patricia Bartlett. *Lizard Care from A to Z.* Barron's Educational Series, 1997.

Case, Russ. *Lizards (Beginning Vivarium Systems).* Advanced Vivarium Systems, 2006.

Cogger, Harold G. *Reptiles and Amphibians of Australia.* CSIRO Publishing, 2014.

Davies, Robert and Valerie Davis. *The Reptile and Amphibian Problem Solver: Practical and Expert Advice on Keeping Snakes and Lizards.* Voyageur Press, 1997.

Gray, John E. and Albert Gunther. *The Lizards of Australia and New Zealand.* Society for the Study of Amphibians and Reptiles, 1995.

Hausschild, Andree and Hubert Bosch. *Bearded Dragons and Frilled Lizards.* Hollywood Import & Export, Inc., 2000.

Marsh, Laura. *National Geographic Readers: Lizards.* National Geographic Children's Books, 2012.

O'Shea, Mark, and Tim Halliday. Smithsonian Handbooks: *Reptiles and Amphibians.* DK Adult, 2002.

Smith, Hobart M. and Herbert S. Zim. *Reptiles and Amphibians (A Golden Guide from St. Martin's Press)*. Golden Guides from St. Martin's Press, 2014.

Sprackland, Robert G. *Guide to Lizards: More Than 300 Essential-to-Know Species (Pocket Professional Guide Series)*. TFH Publications, Inc. 2010.

Vosjoli, Phillipe de. *The Lizard Keeper's Handbook*. Advanced Vivarium Systems, 2007.

Wilson, Steve. *Australian Lizards: A Natural History*. CSIRO Publishing, 2012.

Index